The Ballad of Robyn Hoodie

Written by Noah Leatherland

©2023 **BookLife Publishing Ltd.**
King's Lynn, Norfolk, PE30 4LS, UK

ISBN 978-1-80505-036-0

All rights reserved. Printed in China.
A catalogue record for this book is
available from the British Library.

The Ballad of Robyn Hoodie
Written by Noah Leatherland
Based on a story by Robin Twiddy
Edited by Kirsty Holmes
Illustrated by Warwick Eede

ABOUT THE AUTHORS

Noah is a lifelong fan of comic books, video games and pro wrestling. Trying to tap into all the things that make these hobbies cool is what drives Noah's writing. Noah was a reluctant reader as a kid (and still is), so he hopes to put a bit more fun and excitement into children's books.

Robin is a lifelong comic book fan whose love for the medium led to it being the topic of his undergraduate dissertation. He is the author of many great BookLife titles, including several entries into the BookLife phonic reader scheme. Robin loves action, adventure and humour and brings these elements together into exciting narratives you won't forget.

ABOUT THE ILLUSTRATOR

Warwick Eede illustrates from his home in Lincolnshire. He also works as a part-time Grammar school art teacher. He loves chilling with the family and eating lasagne while listening to the Ramones. His favourite film is Jaws.

CHAPTER 1
Pay to Play

To Robyn, Sherwood Primary didn't look that different to her old school, or the one before that, or the one before that. There were still a few minutes before the school day started, so Robyn figured she might as well play a little before the bell rang. But things were different at Sherwood Primary. Robyn wandered over to the slide. She gripped the cold metal bars and put her foot on the first step, ready to climb up.

A rude voice cut her off, "Pay to play!" Robyn looked over her shoulder and spotted a large boy looming over her.

"What?" said Robyn. The boy rolled his eyes and let out a huff.

"If you want to play," he leaned in, "you've got to pay." His breath reeked of cheese and onion. "What sweets have you got?"

"None for you," Robyn replied. The boy grabbed Robyn's wrist and dragged her off the steps.

"Pay to play," he grunted, pushing Robyn to the floor. Robyn knew a bully when she saw one.

"Fine. I'll go find somewhere else to play," Robyn said as she clambered up to her feet, dusting the dirt off her new uniform.

"Good luck with that!" the bully laughed.

As Robyn walked away, another boy approached the slide. Robyn watched as he passed, his head hanging low and his hands clutching his bag.

"What have you got for us today?" the bully said, rubbing his hands. He snatched the boy's bag and peered inside. "Fruit!?" the bully sneered, "that's not gonna cut it, kid!"

"Please! I don't have enough pocket money for any more sweets!" the boy squeaked. The bully turned the bag upside down and a pair of bananas tumbled onto the concrete.

Robyn saw this happening. Her teeth

clenched and her hands balled into fists. There was nothing she hated more than a bully.

"Fruit is worthless!" the bully yelled, raising a foot. He stamped on one of the bananas. A pale goo exploded out of the yellow fruit, coating the poor boy. The bully lifted his foot to do it again.

"So much for not causing any trouble on my first day," Robyn thought, starting to run towards the bully. Her shoulder struck the bully in the middle of the chest. He flew off his feet and landed in a muddy puddle with a SPLASH!

"I'm going to get you for that!" the bully screamed, wiping the mud off of his face.

"Yeah? You and what army?" Robyn replied. The bully pulled a whistle out of his pocket and brought it to his lips. He sucked in a big breath and blew into it until his cheeks turned red.

The whole playground seemed to pause. Kids shuffled away from Robyn and the muddy bully. Footsteps scuffed across the playground behind Robyn, getting louder and louder. Robyn turned to see more bullies…and they were heading straight for her!

CHAPTER 2
A Friendly Face

Robyn's feet beat hard against the concrete, doing their absolute best to put some distance between her and the bullies. What kind of school is this? Gangs of bullies roaming the playground? Paying with sweets to play? But Robyn couldn't think about how strange this new school was for long.

Her stomach turned just thinking about what the bullies might do if they caught her. The muscles in her legs begged her to stop but her heart kept on thudding in her chest. Robyn's lungs burned with each breath she took, pushing her body to the limit to stay away from the gang chasing her.

Robyn felt a hand take hold of her collar. Was this it? Had the bullies caught her? In an instant Robyn's feet had left the floor and she was pulled through a bush into somewhere dark and green. Her eyes locked with another girl's. The mystery girl raised a finger to her lips.

"Where is she?" barked the muddy bully.

"She can't have gone far!" came another voice. The group of bullies ran off, their footsteps growing quieter and quieter. Robyn finally caught her breath and wiped the sweat from her forehead. She was safe…for now.

"Thank you," Robyn whispered. "Where are we? Who are you?"

"Sherwood Forest. It's my favourite place in the world" she replied. The bush sat in a gap in the playground wall, rows of thick trees stretching beyond. It was definitely a good spot to hide from bullies. "I'm sorry your first day isn't going well. They call me Little Gen. They think it's funny because I am so tall, but I like it."

Little Gen reached out and moved some of the branches, creating a gap for the girls to look out of.

"There are some things you are going to need to know," Gen said, pointing across the playground. "Starting with Norbert."

Gen pointed to a boy sat on a throne in the middle of the playground. His lips were stained with chocolate, empty sweet packets scattered by his feet. Candy of all sorts had turned his tongue a slimy green.

Just as he finished eating one bag of sweets, he quickly opened another to feast on. He was surrounded by a crew of bullies, passing them a few sweets but keeping most for himself.

"He calls himself the King of the Playground," Gen said, a grim look on her face. "You have to pay him in sweets to do anything here."

The bell rang for lessons to begin. The two girls climbed out of the bush as the rest of the children lined up to head inside. It was time for Robyn's first class. Could her day get any stranger?

CHAPTER 3
THE KING'S COURT

Robyn sat in the middle of the classroom, a few rows from the front of the room. The other children's work decorated the walls. As Robyn looked from picture to picture, one name kept jumping out. Norbert. Norbert. Norbert. Norbert.

The knot in her stomach was loosened by her new friend Gen sitting beside her. Ahead of her, she saw Norbert, the King of the Playground, sat in the front row. She could smell the sugar coming off him from her seat. His minions sat around him all slumped down in their chairs, giggling to themselves.

The teacher's pen squeaked across the whiteboard, leaving a word in big black letters for everyone to see.

HEROES

"Class, what makes someone a hero?" the teacher said as they turned to face the children. Hands shot up into the air all over the room. However, the teacher had already decided who to ask. "Norbert, you always have such good answers. What makes a hero?"

"You need to help people. Heroes risk everything to help others," he answered, sitting up straight, a smug grin on his sweet-stained face.

"Exactly right!" chirped the teacher. "You are such a good student, Norbert." As the teacher turned to write on the whiteboard, Norbert looked around at the rest of the class, loving the attention. Robyn's brain tried to piece it all together.

"He's got them all fooled," Gen whispered. "All the teachers think he's the best student ever. He can get away with anything."

Class soon finished and Robyn was back on the playground for break time. She heard a few children playing on the slide and swings, having handed over their sweets to the king's goons. Elsewhere, other children sat by themselves, too poor to play.

As soon as Norbert left the classroom, he transformed back into the mean bully he truly was. His innocent smile turned into a gross grin as he sat on his throne. He tossed more sour candies into his mouth, laughing as his minions brought him more sweets. Robyn and Gen watched as another unlucky boy was brought kicking and screaming to Norbert's throne.

"So, you wanted to play without paying, eh?" Norbert hissed as he snapped his sugary

fingers. His bullies snatched the boy's bag and reached inside. The boy looked on in horror as they pulled out all the sweets he had been hiding. "What's this then?" the king boomed. He looked to his minions. "Give him the Atomic Wedgie!"

The colour drained from Robyn's face. Not the Atomic Wedgie. She couldn't think of anything worse. Gen hid her eyes behind her hands, but Robyn marched forward. The bullies gathered around the boy like a pack of wolves as Norbert watched with glee. They closed in, ready to strike.

"OWWWWWWWWWWWWWW!"

Norbert's laughter stopped. That wasn't

the boy, that was one of his goons! Robyn had gripped the waistband of the biggest bully's undies and pulled them up to the sky. Her arms flexed tight, dishing out the hardest wedgie the playground had ever seen. The bully's feet raised off the ground before Robyn let go, leaving him in a pile on the floor.

Another of the king's goons swung their

bag at Robyn. She ducked out of the way and the bag smashed a third bully in the stomach. A fourth minion rushed at Robyn, but a well-placed foot tripped him, sending them flying into the rest of the goons. Robyn was the last kid standing.

Robyn locked eyes with Norbert. "Who do you think you are?"

"I am the King of the Playground!" he cried, rising from his throne, his voice echoing across the school.

"You're not a king. You're a bully," Robyn snapped, putting a finger in his face. "I am not afraid of bullies."

"You will be," Norbert snapped. "Let's do this!"

Norbert charged at Robyn, and Robyn charged back. But, before they could fight, Norbert dropped to his knees and hid his face in his hands. Robyn could not understand why he was suddenly so scared.

"Get up and fight me, you coward!" Robyn shouted at the trembling king. A tall shadow appeared over the two of them.

Norbert peeked through his fingers, and a nasty smirk stretched across his face. A hand landed on Robyn's shoulder.

"You nasty child! Leave that sweet boy alone." Robyn knew that voice. She looked behind her and saw her teacher. "Your first day and you're already causing trouble."

"Me?" Robyn said. "No, it was–"

The teacher didn't let her finish. "Come inside with me. Now."

Robyn was led back into the classroom, every eye on the playground watching. She looked back and saw Norbert and his thugs back to their feet, high fiving each other. The king stuck out his green tongue and got something from his pocket.

"Say cheese, new girl!" he grinned, holding up his phone.

SNAP!

Robyn stood at the whiteboard all alone, her hand starting to cramp as she finished writing another line.

I will not hurt those who are weaker than me.

None of this felt right. Why was she the one getting punished? Can't the teachers see how Norbert bullies everyone on the playground? As Robyn started another squeaky line on the whiteboard, there was a tap on the window. It was Gen. Something was wrong.

"You are in so much trouble," Gen told her new friend.

"I know. I have twenty more lines to write," Robyn frowned.

"Not that..." Gen murmured. She took her phone and on the screen was the photo Norbert had taken of Robyn. There were some words added to it.

WANTED!

ROBYN LEA LOCKS

REWARD: ONE 'BUMBAG' OF SWEETS

BY ORDER OF THE KING OF THE PLAYGROUND

"He's sent it out to everyone in school," Gen said.

"He can't do this!" Robyn gasped. "I mean, no one is going to turn me in for a few sweets... right?"

Gen didn't look very hopeful.

Robyn was allowed back onto the playground that afternoon, the sun bright in her eyes as she stepped outside again. This time it felt... different. All the kids were looking right at her. As Robyn and Gen wandered onto the playground, the staring kids came closer and closer.

"We are so sorry...," said one.

"We're so poor," said a second, stepping closer.

"You know we can't do anything without sweets…," said another sad face.

"Gen?" Robyn called out, but her friend had vanished.

Everywhere she looked, Robyn saw another desperate face. She tried to step away but more sad faces blocked her path. Robyn couldn't see a way out, she was surrounded. Kids at the back of the crowd started to cough and splutter. A cloud of dust rose in the air, heading towards Robyn. Gen burst through the crowd, placing herself between Robyn and the desperate children. She tossed the fistful of sand she had collected from the sandpits, creating a smoke screen.

"RUN!" Gen shouted, taking her friend by the hand. The girls sprinted back to the bush, hiding in Sherwood Forest once again. "What are we going to do, Robyn? We can't hide in the forest every break time."

Robyn peeked through the bush, making sure none of the other kids had followed them. "Don't worry, I have an idea."

Later that night, Robyn was in her bedroom. She thought about how exhausting her first day at Sherwood Primary had been. She had been chased all over the playground and made plenty of enemies, as well as a friend. But she had a plan to make tomorrow different.

"Come on...where is it?" she muttered, rummaging around under her bed. Her hands soon found the dusty leather handle she was after. She dragged out a ratty briefcase and opened it up. "I didn't think I would need these again," Robyn thought as she opened the case. Inside it sat a bright green hoodie and a peashooter. If her plan worked, Norbert wouldn't be king for much longer.

CHAPTER 5
Steal From the Rich...

Robyn arrived at school the next morning, the green hoodie draped over her school uniform. Her hands were hidden away in the pocket, clutching the peashooter that had been stashed away under her bed. Norbert and his bullies were not going to be messing with her today.

Robyn scanned the playground, looking for somewhere to start freeing the other kids from Norbert's control. Four bullies sprang into sight, carrying a bag heaving with sweets. A cunning smile flashed across Robyn's face.

As the bullies approached, Robyn scrambled up one of the trees that surrounded the playground. She steadied herself in the branches, pulled the peashooter from her pocket and delicately loaded it with peas. She brought it to her lips, ready to open fire. Now, Robyn just had to wait for the bullies to walk into her trap.

"Looks like a big haul today!" cackled one of the bullies. "Come on, let's get all this to the secret stash…"

POP!

"Ow!" another one yelped.

POP! POP! POP!

Robyn grinned as the bullies started to panic. Hidden in the leaves, she puffed into her peashooter and shot another load of peas at the bullies. They cried in pain as pea after pea landed, each one feeling like a bee sting.

"Where are they coming from?" one of Norbert's minions shouted. They started looking around for the shooter. Robyn quickly pulled her hood up. The tree's leaves matched the colour of her green hoodie. Even when the bullies looked right at her, they had no idea she was there. The more they panicked, the more peas Robyn blew out of her peashooter.

POP! POP! POP! POP! POP!

The peas hit them all over their arms and legs. Sore, red spots rose up all over their skin.

"Let's get out of here!" the bullies screamed, throwing up their arms and running away.

Robyn climbed down to the playground, the bullies' whimpers fading away in the distance. She rushed over to the bag they dropped and looked inside. Her eyes lit up with packets and wrappers of all colours and shapes. Sweets, sours, chocolates, gummies, fudge, taffy, a whole bag full!

"Robyn!" said a familiar voice. She looked up from the bag and saw Gen, a bright smile on her face. "That was incredible! You really showed them bullies!"

As well as Robyn's new friend, plenty of other children had seen what Robyn had just done. They shuffled over to Robyn and the bag, their eyes twinkling with hope as they moved from Robyn's hooded face to the bag of sweets and back. Robyn and Gen looked across at the crowd of quiet children and gave each other a nod.

"Dig in, everyone!" Gen cheered, grabbing a handful of sweets and tossing them into the crowd. The children's begging faces turned into wide, beaming smiles. Robyn couldn't help but giggle along as she passed out the sugary treats. The kid's delighted cheers filled the air, bringing back some of the joy Norbert had stolen from them all.

"Thank you… um…" a boy started to say, chocolate already all over his face. "… what was your name?"

"Oh, you can call me…" Robyn began, but Gen interrupted with a proud smile.

"Robyn Hoodie! Her name is Robyn Hoodie!" The thankful children all cheered her new name, so pleased to have their sweets back.

Over the next few days, wherever Norbert's goons went, Robyn was there with her peashooter. As the bullies ran from Robyn's rain of peas, Gen was at the ready to swoop in and collect the bags they dropped. The more this happened, the angrier Norbert became. He sent out more wanted posters with better rewards, but the other children refused to stop Robyn. She was becoming a hero to them. The king was furious. He had had enough.

"Whoever captures the Green Hood and brings her to me will be rewarded beyond their sweetest dreams," he shouted from the top of his throne. "They will become second-in-command, answering only to me!"

With all the other kids behind her, Robyn knew it was time to end Norbert's reign once and for all. She had one more plan in mind. The king had no idea what was coming.

CHAPTER 6
...Give to the Poor

The next day, Robyn was ready to put her grand plan into action. She walked onto the playground once again, pulling the green hoodie's strings tight and rolling up her sleeves. She strolled through the middle of the playground, her heart thudding in her chest. She waited for it…

"There she is!" came a shout from one of Norbert's bullies. He grabbed his whistle and blew into it, his finger stretched out and pointing right at Robyn. Norbert's goons from all over the playground rushed over, gathering round as Robyn stared them down. They all wanted to be Norbert's second-in-command. To do that, they'd need to capture the girl in the green hoodie.

The bullies glared at her. Robyn stood her ground. The playground fell silent.

"Here goes nothing," Robyn muttered. Her shoes scraped the concrete as she turned, bursting out into a sprint away from Norbert's minions. They all darted after her as if a starting pistol had fired, a stampede of bullies storming across the playground, hot on Robyn's heels. Robyn's arms pumped along with her legs, her whole body dedicated to keeping away from these bullies. She led them past the swings, past the slide, past the sandpit, past the entrance to Sherwood Forest, and finally around the corner of the school.

"That's a dead-end!" a bully shouted out. "We've got her now!"

The bullies followed close behind and spotted Robyn, but much more too. Robyn kept running, into a whole crowd of children in green hoodies. With their hoods up and faces hidden, Robyn blended into the crowd with ease. Everywhere the bullies looked, there was a green hoodie.

"NOW!"

The crowd of hoodies reached into their pockets and pulled out water balloons of every colour. SPLATSPLATSPLATSPLATSPLAT! The bullies screamed as the rubber exploded on their skin and soaked them in icy water. SPLATSPLATSPLATSPLATSPLATSPLAT! The onslaught of cold water seemed to go on forever. Just as a bright red balloon landed

right on a head, there were three more already in the air. SPLATSPLATSPLATSPLATSPLAT! The wet rubber clung to their skin, the water filling their shoes.

"Stop!" Robyn ordered, stepping out from the crowd. "Give it up! You have no power over these kids anymore. Together, we are more powerful than you!" Poking out from around the corner, Norbert's eyes locked with Robyn's.

"The king has no power!" Robyn yelled. Norbert turned and ran. Robyn led her green army after him, balloons streaming through the air towards the king. She chased him into the caretaker's shed. Robyn pulled the door open and revealed a sight none of the kids on the playground would ever forget. There was the king, laying on a massive pile of sweets.

"My secret stash! It's all mine!" Norbert cried as he stuffed as much of the sweet hoard into his mouth as he could. "You can't have it back! I took it fair and square!" he squealed like a pig. He chomped and chewed on all the sweets his mouth could hold.

"What is going on?" a voice asked. Robyn turned, it was her teacher. This time, the teacher saw what was really going on. "Norbert...you bad boy!" You're coming with me!" The teacher peeled Norbert off his sticky stash and dragged him out of the shed.

"Everyone! Help yourselves! It's all yours," Robyn said as she and Gen stepped toward Norbert's stash. They scooped up the sweets and dished them out to all the children they had been stolen from. The kids all cheered Robyn Hoodie's name as they were reunited with their sweets. Just like the chocolate around his face, Norbert's control of the playground melted away. The king was no more, and Robyn had become the hero of Sherwood Primary.